AF415280

Psychology for beginners

The basics of psychology explained simply - understanding and manipulating people

Claudia Sonnenbeck

CONTENT

Introduction to psychology

Psychology is a subject with wide and partially unexplored horizons. The psychological well-being of an individual is in fact dependent on every single influence. Starting in the womb, continuing with education, hobbies, views, knowledge, feelings and learned values. These influences provide namely for positive development or also for negative development. These opposites of the positive and negative development describe thereby roughly seen finally the psychology. This tries to explain behaviors of an individual and offers the possibility to overcome fears, for example.

To ensure a good introduction to the subject, it is important to mention that one groups the generic term of psychology into many detailed aspects and subtopics. In this context, new findings regularly contribute to the development and progress of psychology. For example, new methods and new therapies are developed through advanced brain research and behavioral observations by compiling statistics.

The term psychology comes from the ancient Greek and means - if translated literally - as much as psychology or the study of the soul. The human senses, i.e. seeing, hearing, smelling, feeling and tasting, are particularly important in this so-called psychology, because these senses help with almost every mental disorder or are one of the first construction sites.

To better understand psychology, with all the topics and areas, the following listed content is helpful. Psychology is very complex, but herewith psychology is explained simply for beginners.

The history of psychology

The history of psychology provides one with an important background knowledge to understand psychology, because many of our therapies today are based on thinking at that time. First of all, psychology can be traced back to the 19th century. At that time, the official establishment of psychology as an independent and scientifically respected field of research happened through the joining of research groups. However, this field of research actually existed *before Christ*. A Greek scholar named Aristotle, who was a philosopher and natural scientist by "profession", wrote a book called "De anima" - "On the Soul" - in which he talks about the soul of man, discusses and conjectures. This book and the discussions of that time were ultimately considered the basis for the scientist and educator Siegmund Freud and his models about the psyche.

Thereby different coinages, as for example the materialism, led to our today's knowledge. In the 19th century, for example, the importance of the sense organs of an individual was already recognized and expanded and improved by our present knowledge. But the psychologists, which consisted of philosophers, physicians and natural scientists, were not always in agreement, of course, which is why many directions in psychology arose at the beginning of the 20th century and even still exist today. However, these different directions will be described and explained in more detail later, but still form the foundations of our psychology today.

Self-test: What is my mental state?

The following is a self-test, which is intended to describe the psychological condition of an individual. It serves as an aid to getting to know oneself better and to take a closer look at the subject. Fifteen statements are now listed in more detail. These statements are based on different personal feelings and behaviors. The test works in such a way that you can give yourself points from 1-10 for each statement. The number one means "Not true" and the number ten means "True". The numbers 2-9 indicate tendencies.

1. I tend to be anxious and nervous.

2. I worry a lot about a lot of different things.

3. I think I can control few things and that plagues me.

4. I have bad and restless sleep.

5. I live a lot in the past.

6. My eating behavior has changed involuntarily.

7. I am often listless and unmotivated.

8. I often prefer to be alone.

9. I am easily irritated and suffer from mood swings.

10. I often feel drained from everyday life.

11. I neglect my family and hobbies.

12. I often have negative thoughts.

13. My energy is missing.

14. My family has already drawn my attention to my behavior.

15. I don't laugh much anymore.

The evaluation of these statements now works very simply. The corresponding individual score is noted down for each statement. The higher the score, the more likely it is that the mental state is definitely not in an ideal state and needs improvement.

In order to approach the ideal state and improve one's own well-being, there are various exercises and methods that contribute to becoming happier and thinking more positively.

Scientific psychology vs. lay psychology

To the psychology belong in the generic term two strictly to differentiate terms. First, the concept of scientific psychology and also the concept of lay psychology.

Lay psychology is also called everyday psychology. It includes findings from psychology, which is not based on scientific criteria and facts. This means that everyday psychology does not set the standards of knowledge on scientific evidence, but is based on common assumptions through similar personal experiences, experiences, stories and more.

Through everyday psychology, myths arose, among other things, in the area of gender stereotypes, in the area of marital status, as well as in the area of age. A widespread myth is that women definitely always have more speech than men and that this is because women always have to communicate and need attention. This is an example from typical everyday psychology. Events that apply more often are reformulated as universally valid and a psychology behind them is sought and suitably restructured.

Above all this happens also if one could disprove myths scientifically, since this is not considered with the everyday psychology. To remain with the same example: The scientific study 6 APSYH01 1 could disprove that women speak more than men. Both men and women speak on average about 16,000 words per day.

The most important differences between everyday psychology and scientific psychology are thus that in everyday psychology myths as well as unreflected statements are generalized without being critically scrutinized. Contradictory claims are made and not scientifically substantiated, data collection is based on coincidences and not on structured statistics and analysis. In scientific psychology, they are verifiable using scientifically designed methods and concepts. Moreover, despite different orientations and paths, researchers often arrive at the same findings and results based on scientific rules and concepts.

The everyday phrase "opposites attract", on the other hand, is not scientifically verifiable, nor is it scientifically testable. The "everyday psychologists" deal with different interpretations and their established theories are not or only badly verifiable and repeatable. Theories, however, are verifiable in reality with scientific methods. However, a present problem in everyday psychology is also that these phrases fit almost every situation and therefore their "correctness" can often be found in the world.

Nevertheless, it should be clear to everyone that psychological inferences do not have a monocausal explanation (single cause), but that human behaviors can have drastic differences. Psychology, as an objective, experimental, and statistics-based natural science, aims to change the control over a person's behavior. Psychology is considered a behavioral science based on methodology and on human experience.

Areas of psychology

Psychology is therefore a behavioral science as well as a natural science, which represents behavior and experience and distinguishes itself with the help of scientific perspectives and methods from the already above described everyday psychology or lay psychology. The acquisition of knowledge in psychology is based on sociocultural, psychological and biological levels and can therefore be divided into different areas or disciplines which are distinguished between *basic **subjects**, applied subjects* and *methodological subjects.*

Starting with the basics, it should be mentioned that within these disciplines a distinction is made between subjects that are also part of other basic subjects and subjects that present basic findings in certain contexts and contexts. The first differentiation, i.e. subjects that are also part of other basic subjects, includes general psychology, biopsychology and psychological methodology. Social psychology, personality psychology, differential psychology and developmental psychology belong to the field of basic knowledge.

General psychology and biological psychology are briefly explained in more detail: General psychology deals with the question of which regularities and connections can be found with regard to the experience and behavior of a person and which commonalities result from this. Aspects such as knowledge, attention, emotions, motivations, perception, learning, cognition and language are dealt with.

Biological psychology, on the other hand, deals with the areas that affect experience and behavior. Aspects such as a person's genetics are studied, but so are anatomy, physiology, brain activity, muscle activity, heart rate, blood pressure, and other aspects that deal with the biology of the human body.

The disciplines of the application areas are very

distinctive and strongly branched with subtopics. Basically, however, one can say that clinical psychology with the topics of neuropsychology and medical psychology, business psychology with the subtopics of industrial psychology including engineering psychology, organizational psychology, industrial psychology, financial psychology, leadership psychology, market psychology including retail psychology, consumer psychology, sales psychology and advertising psychology. Other areas of application are educational psychology, peace psychology, community psychology, gerontological psychology, health psychology, media psychology, military psychology, music psychology, political psychology, and legal psychology with the subtopics criminal psychology and forensic psychology. But also areas such as religious psychology, school psychology, sports psychology, environmental psychology and traffic psychology belong to the fields of application.

The methodological subjects are also subdivided in a complex way. One of the most important aspects and umbrella terms is the psychological methodology with the subtopics meta-analysis, philosophy of science, experimental methodology, evaluation research, ethics, mathematics, computer science and mathematical psychology. The aspect of mathematics still has the subtopic stochastics, which deals with statistics, game theory, combinatorics and probability theory/calculation. Psychological diagnostics forms the second important umbrella term in this area.

Currents of psychology

The currents of psychology include 5 themes, which are very different. These include behaviorism, depth psychology, Gestalt psychology, cognitive psychology and humanistic psychology.

Behaviorism took its origin in humans at the beginning of the twentieth century. This current is fundamentally concerned with a triggered stimulus and the subsequent reaction of an individual. The interest was particularly related to learning behavior and learning processes. These processes, respectively the different behaviors, can be negative as well as positive. The scheme that precisely describes the exploration of stimulus and behavior is called stimulus-response scheme. Between the nineteenth and the twentieth century, a physiologist had made the first researches of this reflex investigation, which was tested, however, first with dogs.

<u>Depth psych</u>ology, on the other hand, is much more concerned with the psychology of man using other methods and approaches. Depth psychology can be divided into three main aspects. The first one describes the methodical analysis of human behavior and human experience. The second aspect describes an established theory in this area, and the third main carrier is the three instances of ego, id, and superego. However, equally important aspects of dream interpretation as well as the explanation of psychological disorders and sexual directions belong to this topic.

Gestalt psychology, on the other hand, views and treats experience and perception as a whole. For this reason, it is also called the theory of perception. People who practice Gestalt psychology therefore always try to find laws or explanations which help one to explain man with his various interpretations. For example, the following questions are addressed:

• Why is it possible to put some things in the background, but others in the focus?

• On what factors does the speed of detections depend?

• Why and why do humans see certain connections between things?

• What factors can make it easier or more difficult to recognize these connections?

Cognitive psychology, or cognitivism, is concerned with the analysis and study of an individual's information processing.

The last current, i.e. Humanistic Psychology, is about individual self-development, self-determination, self-realization and more. The basic assumption of this current is based on the idea that healthy personalities develop with this form of psychology.

Physiological psychology

Physiological psychology attempts to explain how emotions, behaviors, as well as changes in consciousness are related to aspects such as breathing, motor function, hormones, circulation, and brain activity. For example, emotions and stress interact to play a significant role in the body. The research focus will be directed toward examining how sensory stimuli are processed. For example, sensing pain can cause the heartbeat to increase and muscles to begin to tense. This reaction also happens, for example, in the psychological disorder "panic attacks." The signal of pain is sent out and the person gets palpitations - he or she gets into the situation and falls into mortal fear.

Psychosomatics

Psychosomatics is also called disease theory or holistic approach, among others. In psychosomatics, processes and interconnections are examined that occur in both a healthy and a sick person through mental abilities. The word is composed of ancient Greek and means soul (psyche) and body (soma).

In psychosomatics, mainly the psychological influences due to somatic actions are investigated and analyzed. In doing so, one tries to identify the origin, which has been transferred to the body by a psychological stimulus. Somatopsychology is the so-called counterpart to psychosomatics. Somatopsychology is the counterpart of psychosomatics, which deals with how the psychological and emotional level suffers as a result of a physical illness. Psychosomatic medicine is the execution and implementation of psychosomatic medicine in a hospital or medical facility. The recognition, prevention, treatment as well as the rehabilitation belong to the basic tasks. This then includes a wide variety of applications: One example is when physical illness is present, such as cancer. Other examples are post-traumatic disorder, stress disorders, personality disorders, eating disorders and many more.

But psychosomatics does not mean that one always necessarily makes a somatic finding. There are also psychological disorders that trigger physical pain without any real risk of concern. A typical example is the psychological disorder "panic attacks". In the case of panic attacks, it can be basically said that the person reacts hypersensitively to certain stimuli and usually dramatizes things. A twinge in the chest is self-diagnosed as an imminent heart attack, yet this "twinge in the chest" is not as real as the individual perceives, nor does it mean that one's life is in danger. For example, if an individual had the first panic attack before an exam, then it is likely that any stimuli that has anything to do with an exam will trigger another panic attack. It could be the sound of a book being opened, the smell of paper, or even holding the same pen. Every stimulus that the body takes in is converted and the body becomes nervous and "makes itself ache". In this case the psychosomatic examination can give information about the subject and one can go as an affected person into a psychological treatment.

The perception of a stimulus and a subsequent reaction is also called a psychosomatic connection. The example of panic attacks is equally appropriate. The feeling of fear, which one feels during a panic attack, causes the adrenal glands of a person to release adrenaline. This release has the consequence that the autonomic nervous system is disturbed and, for example, digestive disorders can be the result. That is why many sayings we used are true. When you're nervous or you have fear and anxiety, you often say, "Something's heavy in my stomach," or even "The fright is running down my limbs." External influences can also make the reaction or consequence worse. For example, constantly falling asleep in front of the television can lead to disturbed sleep patterns and a sleep disorder can be the resulting cause. But toxins such as alcohol, tobacco or drugs in general can also have psychosomatic effects.

Perceptual Psychology

In the psychology of perception, the so-called <u>subjective</u> part of <u>perception</u> is studied. In order to better understand the psychology of perception, it is important to know that we speak between objective and subjective relations between stimuli and their sensations. Objective perception describes that healthy people (i.e. without visual impairment, hearing impairment or similar) - since they all have the same sensory organs - perceive a stimulus in the same way. Thereby the subjective perception is the one, which determines in the final effect, how this received stimulus is interpreted. So, in the psychology of perception, the part is studied and explained that is not explained by science, but by our basic anatomy.

PERCEPTION THEORY

For the explanation of the perceptions there are different theories which should give information about it. One theory is the theory of Hermann von Helmholtz.

This theory was established in 1866 and states that the experience that an individual makes or has made is decisive for the view of his environment. According to Hermann von Helmholtz, experience contributes decisively to our view of the environment. An individual unconsciously uses his experiences to judge and conclude about what he perceives. This "unconscious inference" ensures that one can perceive so briskly in one's familiar environment because one needs few cue stimuli. In an unfamiliar environment, however, this can at the same time lead to the fact that processes taking place in the environment are misinterpreted by the unfamiliar situations and one thus feels uncomfortable or even causes discomfort to the people around oneself.

Another theory of perception is James J. Gibson's ecological theory of perception. Gibson's theory examines three basic factors for analysis. The first factor describes the factor of the exact analysis of the information in the environment. The second factor describes the "consideration of the activity of living beings" and the third aspect describes the "specification of the perceptual offers of the world according to the species specificity of the respective living beings of interest". In examining these three aspects, it was found that it is not the individual stimuli that cause an individual to take something in, but that it is in the variety of invariants over time and motion. In addition, the action offer also plays an important role in this theory. For example, the action offer of an escalator is perceived differently depending on the species.

GESTALT PSYCHOLOGY

Another important subtopic in the psychology of perception is Gestalt psychology. This describes the experience as a wholeness. In Gestalt psychology there are the so-called Gestalt laws, which were formulated in 1923. The first law is called the law of proximity and means that elements which do not have a large distance from each other are perceived as belonging together.

The second law is called the law of similarity. This states that elements and objects which are similar to each other are more likely to be classified by an individual as belonging together than elements which cause clear dissimilarity.

Following gives the law of good shape, which states that an individual prefers to perceive shapes that have a simple structure.

Another law is the law of good continuation or also called the law of continuous lines. This law describes that when you see two lines forming an X, you don't assume that they are two lines with a kink, but that they are two straight lines that just cross each other.

Another law is the law of closure. This means that an individual prefers to perceive structures that are closed and do not appear open and unclosed.

Another law is the law of common fate, which describes that it is preferred to perceive something that moves in the same direction. This can be one element, two elements or even several elements. This law was the last one which existed at that time until Stephen Palmer formulated three more Gestalt laws in 1990.

These laws were named as the law of common region, law of simultaneity as well as the law of connected elements.

Here, the first law, i.e., the law of common region, describes that elements that are located in demarcated areas are more likely to be perceived and felt by someone as belonging together than when this is not so.

The law of simultaneity describes that simultaneous changes are equally more likely to be classified as belonging together. And the last law, the law of connected elements, describes that connected elements are perceived as a whole and unified object.

If you know these laws, you can notice that these laws are also often exploited in our world. An example of this is the media. Either media use these laws to reconstruct a "connected and unified feeling" or to deliberately emphasize something, which means that these laws are broken on purpose.

For example, the color red is the complementary color to green, which means that if something is in the color red on a green background, the human brain perceives this more intensely. But this breaks the law of similarity. But these Gestalt laws are also applied in other areas.

SENSORY PERCEPTION

Another important point in the field of perceptual psychology is, of course, sensory perception. As is well known, a human being has five senses, which enable the following: seeing, smelling, hearing, tasting and feeling. In the technical language one speaks with "seeing" of visual perception with the eye. Visual stimuli are perceived with the eye, such as brightness, contrast, colors, outlines, shapes, three-dimensionality as well as movements and other impressions.

Hearing" is also referred to as auditory perception with the ear. The ear picks up sound, tones and noises and has the ability to identify the distance of sounds as well as the direction. Auditory perception can also be activated by the sense of touch in the case of very loud sounds, as the vibrations can be felt. In addition, however, the ear likewise has the ability to control a person's sense of balance, thus giving an individual the ability to grasp control of movement.

The sense of touch is described as tactile perception and helps humans feel touch with the help of cold and heat receptors. However, a distinction is made between the following two subsystems: The first aspect is depth sensitivity. This describes the perception of the body limbs and the related body posture. Here, instead of a single organ, a larger quantity of receptors is made responsible for the reception of stimuli. This is summarized under the term "muscle sense". In addition, the body's own perception of its own organs also belongs to this aspect.

The second aspect is tactile perception, which is used to feel temperature, vibrations, touch and pressure. The sensory organ, which leads to the fact that one can take up all these stimuli, is thereby the skin.

The sense of smell is described as olfactory perception and is picked up with the nose. The detection of odors is strongly associated with emotions in the brain and is therefore often a companion in therapy. The sense of smell is also described as Gustatory Perception and is picked up by the tongue, which carries various taste receptors that help identify food, chemicals and more.

In the psychology of perception, the senses play an enormously important role, because without these senses a person could firstly not perceive at all and secondly the different senses offer an individual many different ways of interpreting situations and are thus significant for decision making.

CLAUDIA SONNENBECK

FIGURE-GROUND-PERCEPTION (EXAMPLE "RUBY CUP" BY WELLHÖGER 1990)

In the field of sensory perception, there is also the concept of figure-ground perception, which is exemplified by a ruby cup. The figure-ground-perception describes the distinction of foreground and background by the individual weighting of the received stimuli. To explain the example: In the picture, one finds a ruby cup depicted in white and, in each case, to the left and right of it in rough shapes and in the color black, people who are symmetrical and looking at each other. The question is whether the cup is perceived first and the black is merely the background, or whether the people are perceived first and the white fades into the background and is not recognized as a cup at all. Through the influx of the various stimuli through the colors and shapes, etc., the brain filters out which impressions seem important and which do not. In the process, the important stimuli are placed in the foreground and the unimportant stimuli are automatically placed in the background.

Personality Psychology

Personality psychology is a field of psychology that generally deals with the personality of an individual. Motives, developments and stimulus reactions characterize this psychology.

THE BIG FIVE PERSONALITY MODEL

The Big-Five Personality Model is a five-factor model from the field of personality psychology, which has existed for a very long time and is still one of the international and recognized models for examining the personality of an individual. The five personality factors are:

- <u>Openness to</u> experience
- <u>Conscientiousness</u>
- <u>Extraversion</u>
- <u>Compatibility</u>
- <u>Neuroticism</u>

The factor openness describes the interest in new experiences, experiences as well as occupations in connection with collected impressions. The factor conscientiousness describes the characteristic of self-control and the characteristic of the perfectionist. Extraversion broadly describes interpersonal behavior. The next factor is called "Agreeableness" and also describes interpersonal behavior. The last factor is neuroticism, which reflects negative emotions and is the counterpart of emotional strength.

BIG-FIVE SELF-TEST: WHAT PERSONALITY DO I HAVE?

An important question that occupies one's mind is the question of one's own personality. In order to filter this out, one must first consider what abilities the various personalities have.

Open people are characterized by:
• Good imagination
• Skillfully classify their feelings
• Interest in public processes
• Curiosity
• Willingness to experiment
• Unconventional behavior
• New is more interesting and better than old and proven

Conscientious individuals are characterized by:
• Organization
• Care
• Reliability
• Superiority and planning

Individuals with extraversion behavior are:

• sociable

• active

• chatty

• optimistic

• warmly

Compatible people have the following characteristics:

• Desire for social acceptance

• You are understanding

• They are benevolent

• You are compassionate

Individuals high in neuroticism are:

• Anxious

• Tense

• Unsafe

• Lay

• Thoughtful

• Hypersensitive to negative emotions

To find out what personality you have now, you should take a closer look at the factors and think carefully about which aspects you are most likely to be attracted to.

HOW CAN YOU CHANGE YOUR CHARACTER / PERSONALITY STRUCTURES?

Basically, you can say that it is possible to change your personality. You can usually see this just by looking back and seeing that you are not the same person in terms of behavior as you were 5 years ago. However, a personality change means a lot of patience, time and discipline. Most of the time it is small quirks or bad habits that you would like to change about yourself, but the time to break the habit is very difficult. You have to pay special attention to your body and listen to it well. But the first and best step of a personality change is the fact to visualize yourself what it means to change your personality or a part of your personality.

Developmental Psychology

Developmental psychology is an important part of psychology and describes the change of experience and behavior in view of the complete life span of a person. In particular, the healthy course of a life is observed and not a period of life that was characterized by illness.

The concept of developsment in this regard is very difficult to explain. In general, however, it can be said that development is understood as the process of emergence and change, and in terms of psychology, development is referred to as three principles. The first thematized principle is the principle of growth, the second is the principle of maturation and the third principle is titled as the principle of learning.

The principle of the growth thematizes thereby above all the change of the body structure and in closer view the form, the size etc.. The expression maturation designates the concrete development of reflexes, instincts or further behaviors, which one had not learned, but one carries in itself in the body with itself.

The last principle, that is, the principle of learning, refers both to the traditional area of conditioning and to the area that includes school learning. The task of developmental psychology is thus to explain why certain changes have occurred, for what reasons the feeling of stability comes, and why there are inter- and intraindividual differences in this respect.

Social Psychology

Social psychology is a subject that occurs both in the field of sociology, but also in the field of psychology. It describes the influence of various social factors as well as experience and behavior. Thus, the thinking and acting as well as the behavior is studied taking into account the social influence.

It is well known that all processes of a human being with regard to behavior, reactions and opinion formation take place under consideration of social norms and one's own state of mind. However, the environment can also influence decisions both consciously and unconsciously. For example, an individual feels much more comfortable in a group of people who move similarly, dress similarly, and have similar interests than in a group that does not meet all these points. This phenomenon occurs because of identification with the social environment.

Social psychology was able to find out that it is always important for an individual to be able to identify and have a pleasant environment in order to develop positive thoughts. This insight helped social psychologists to actively help, for example, in alleviating pain and combating phobias and fears.

However, the research area of social psychology includes many and various fields. Examples are social perception, social cognition, the construction of the self, and attitudes.

Social perception deals with how collected information is received and interpreted by observing the environment. Subtopics such as the attribution theories, the theory of the corresponding conclusions as well as the covariation theory belong to the generic term of the social perception. The attribution theories thematize the explanations for the behavior of people. The theory of the corresponding conclusions assumes thereby, "that observers from an observed behavior on appropriate intentions conclude". The last theory, i.e. the covariation theoryexplains the different and individual assessments of people in relation to an observed situation and action.

The area of <u>social cognition</u> comprises the further superordinate topic of social psychology and serves for the explanation of thought processes. The social cognition is there to find out why and why an action and reaction can be influenced due to a social aspect. In this process, a basic distinction is made between two different processes, namely between the automatic and the controlled (thinking) process. An automatic process is described as one that happens automatically and subconsciously without intention, without disturbing the cognitive processes that take place simultaneously. A controlled process, on the other hand, is one that is brought about intentionally and occurs consciously in a person.

Following there is also in the field of social psychology the construction of one's self.

In this theme, various causes are analyzed that are related to the individual. The big question of "why" and the big question of "wherefrom" in relation to the self-knowledge of a person is worked out in this topic. However, central questions are not only the origin and the "why?", but also concepts such as self-concept, self-schemata and self-esteem are essential aspects that play a role in the topic "construction of one's self".

We continue with the topic of "<u>attitudes</u>". This topic is understood to mean that an individual evaluates various things such as groups, fringe groups, behavior, opinions as well as but also people in his social environment. This is because the inner attitude has an enormous influence on how a person thinks and acts as an individual, since attitudes influence perceptions. In this topic, the multicomponent model of attitude is a common model, which states that the definition of the term attitude is that a person tries to make an evaluation of an object based on <u>cognitive</u>, <u>affective</u> and behavioral foundations. In this context, the interplay between attitude and behavior is very important. Because as attitude researchers say, attitudes can predict a person's behavior.

Other areas that social psychology deals with would include emotions, social roles, sense of justice, verbal and nonverbal communication, aggression, prejudice, and much more.

Advertising Psychology

Advertising psychology describes the effect on people of advertising, which is received through various ways and means. The advertising psychology serves for the purpose of the active influence. It is to help thus and/or it is to cause that the customer buys something. The recognition effect often determines the purchase. This recognition can happen by a slogan, in addition, by a certain, loud melody, which flows directly into one's head, if one sees the product advertised thereby. So it is not only a matter of associating certain stimuli with the advertising campaigns that are generally running, but it is also a matter of achieving a certain recognition effect as a salesperson. For this purpose, repetitions are very important, so that the slogan, the melody, etc. are also catchy and sooner or later get stuck in the head of an individual. Thereby it is even completely the same whether one likes the melody or the slogan is varied. Fact and goal is only that it must remain in the head and the product gets attention.

Another method of advertising psychology works with classical conditioning. This means trying to encourage people to buy a product by giving them regular rewards. An example of this is advertising a good that everyone wants. Protein-rich oatmeal, for example, is said to be ideal for breakfast. So they advertise that eating this product will make you fitter and healthier, guaranteed. Everyone wants to be fitter and healthier, so they buy the product with the confidence that it will help them. There is a procedure that can be simply called <u>AIDAS</u> for short. AIDAS stands for 1. attention, 2. interest, 3. desire, 4. action, 5. satisfaction and addresses the most important aspects for a good and promising advertisement:

1. Attracting attention is the key to gaining potential customers
2. The interest to want to deal with the product must be aroused
3. The sensing of a desire to buy must be ensured
4. The advertised product should be purchased
5. The customer should receive a purchase confirmation and be happy with his decision to have bought this product. The customer should be so happy and convinced that he wants to buy the product again and again.

This means that after a successful and happy purchase, the consumer's process in relation to the product is as follows: Advertising -> Purchase -> Advertising -> Post-purchase -> Advertising -> Post-purchase etc.

Another essential heat technique is the so-called PPPP. This means "1. picture, 2. promise,3. prove and 4. push".

This advertising technique includes compliance with the following points:

1. Pictorial visualizations for illustration
2. The advertisement should contain a guarantee or promise
3. The promise must also be proven by recognized facts
4. A call to action must be given

The last point to consider in terms of advertising psychology is <u>USP</u>, also short for "unique selling proposition". This abbreviation is merely intended to mean, broadly speaking, that advertising slogans should be kept catchy and simple.

So, in short, we can say on the subject of advertising psychology that advertising has an enormous impact on the human psyche and there are very many tricks that encourage people to buy something and believe something.

Sports Psychology

Sports psychology is a therapy that uses sports to help identify certain behavioral patterns. In addition, this therapy should help to solve problems or the goal is to counteract problems with the help of sports. Sport is considered in medicine and psychology as a means that unites mind and body. For example, one can let pent-up aggression run free through boxing or train one's own endurance through cardio and thus "exhaust" the body. In short, sports have sonnen proven to help people become happy. Sport initially gives you self-confidence. You constantly have the feeling that you have achieved something and give yourself a good self-esteem. You don't have to set high goals, because even 30 minutes of walking can be enough.

In addition, scientists together with psychologists were able to find out that regular exercise leads to better sleep. First of all, because the cardiovascular system becomes better, and secondly, because the body through exercise is more likely to manage to transport you to the deep sleep phase and rem sleep phase. Sleep is indispensable for the human body. First of all, for the reason that at some point our body is very powerless and our muscles need time off, but equally also so that things from the past and things that have happened during the day can be processed.

However, if one does not get into the deep sleep phase and also not into the rem sleep phase sensibly, then the brain cannot process certain things and people become unhappy and quickly feel physically weak and exhausted. This feeling can then be counteracted with the method of sports therapy and thus not only treat yourself, but also have the opportunity to find out where exactly the problems are. Because also in this therapy, even if it is based on sports, it is important to filter out the origin of the problem, to recognize it and then to fight it.

Positive psychology

Positive psychology describes the treatment of positive aspects such as happiness, optimism, security and much more. The focus of this topic is on character strengths, which include aspects such as individual cognitive strength, emotional strength and humanity, but also civil strength such as justice, fairness and responsibility. This form of psychology is often applied in corporate practice, for example, in the field of "positive leadership", in the field of education, as well as in education. Positive psychology is essential for every human being, because it makes you feel good.

However, you can also apply positive psychology to yourself by always keeping certain aspects and phrases in mind:

10 USEFUL AFFIRMATIONS

Useful affirmations in the area of positive thinking would include the following:

1. I can take my life into my own hands.
2. Other people love and respect me for who I am.
3. I am valuable.
4. I accept myself as I am.
5. I forgive myself.
6. I have fun in life.
7. I am lovable.
8. I am valuable.
9. I love my body.
10. I deserve perfect health.

LEARN POSITIVE THINKING EXERCISES

But you can also learn positive thinking through

various exercises. For example, you can protect yourself from a crisis or better cope with a crisis.

In order to learn positive thinking, one must first visualize where exactly the problems are located and how exactly the problem feels. It is important to try to be as detailed as possible in the description, as this will lead to a better end result. After a person has made this clear, he can perform the exercises that will help to think more positively. Basic are so-called mindfulness exercises that can be integrated into one's everyday life so that one learns to think more positively, respectively. Mindfulness exercises include, among others, meditation tasks.

Whether a person thinks positively or not has something to do with a person's resilience, i.e. their inner emotional strength. How well developed this is varies from person to person, because it is developed through upbringing, experiences and external circumstances in childhood. In order to think positively, however, it is important to strengthen one's resilience, as this is the key to positive thinking. For this, however, many factors are important to keep in mind as a negative-thinking person: These include the factors of acceptance, positive emotions, optimism, positive self-perception, conviction of control, self-efficacy

expectation, and the social network factor. These factors are all covered in resilient people. Resilient people,
for example, accept change and do not try to always
fight change.

They have accepted that change is part of life and
inevitable. So it is easier for such people, when something happens that causes negative thoughts, to get out
of the "low" again. Resilient people accept that there is
not a solution to everything in the world, and are
equally at peace with that as they are with an answer.
Other skills such as the ability to sort out one's feelings
and know one's mood are also part of this.

They characterize themselves with optimism and
through the ability to restructure one's inner beliefs,
they obtain new beliefs that can make one happier.
These aspects, but also numerous others, are many
building sites that must be worked on to ensure more
positive thinking, but are all coverable through exercises.

Meditation and mindfulness exercises, in which
one consciously pays attention to one's own mind and
mindfully and consciously takes in influences with
one's senses, especially help one to be at one with oneself. Otherwise, it is the active restructuring of beliefs
and the internalization of the new, as well as the

conscious and active cultivation of social contacts that help one to think more positively. Good relationships and positive inner beliefs make you happy, and it has been proven that regular meditation exercises restructure your brain to make you happier.

Motivational Psychology

The motivation psychology is a form of psychology, which deals particularly with the effects with the behavior, as soon as an individual is motivated, and examines, which motives an individual needs, in order to attain the needed motivation. In doing so, motivational psychology fundamentally talks about 4 findings that are considered as a guide.

The first insight is that motivation is the key to understanding human behavior. Only when you, as an outside person, are aware of what motives or motivational motives are present, can you understand certain behaviors. An example of this is a person who grew up in great poverty and now in their new life owns a lot of old items and hoards more and more things, even though the person is financially stable. If you didn't know the background, you wouldn't understand why the person doesn't just throw things in the trash. But after you know what motivation drives him to do this, namely the fear of losing everything again, then you look at the situation with a different view, because you can understand the behavior.

The second insight is the aspect that states that motives are initially always linked to a specific goal. At the same time, we are not always conscious of the goals, but they are there in any case. An unconscious goal, which one pursues, often turns out during communication, for example when one unconsciously wants to animate someone to change his decision by the tone of voice. But of course, these motives can also be quite real, such as working a lot of overtime because you want to finance a vacation.

The third insight includes the point that the nature of a motive often determines whether one succeeds or fails. Most of the time, people fail to achieve their goals because their own motivation gets in the way. This often happens when someone sets other people's goals as their own without actively thinking about what they want for themselves.

The fourth and final insight describes the way people deal with frustration. Because there are different ways of dealing with it, which can be decisive for the success of an individual. Indeed, the reason for failure to achieve goals often comes from the fact that the appropriate way of dealing with frustration has not been learned. The very first difficulties cause one to give up motivation instead of viewing the difficulty as a renewed challenge. Conversely, this also means that an individual is given the opportunity to benefit from a difficult phase. Of course, it makes sense to break away from one or the other goal, but every person knows from the bottom of his heart what he really wants.

In addition, there are some basic forms of motivation that determine the probability of achieving a desired goal. Psychologists distinguish between four *basic dimensions of* motivation:

The type of motivation also plays a role in determining whether a goal is achieved with a high probability or not. Psychologists usually distinguish between four basic dimensions of motivation:

The first dimension is intrinsic or extrinsic motivation. Extrinsic motivation describes motivation that comes from outside and has nothing to do with the actual goal. A classic example of this can be found in children at school. The parents offer the child a material reward, provided that good grades are written. The child's goal in learning is often less the good grade, but rather the reward. The motivation to learn then came from the outside. In contrast to this is Intrinsic Motivation, which describes the motivation that comes from within. This motivation can, for example, take the form of curiosity, a thirst for knowledge or general interest.

In this first dimension, studies have found that intrinsic motivation is stronger and more long-lasting in an individual than extrinsic motivation. Extrinsic motivation is usually due insofar as tasks arise that have little to do with one's own needs or interests. For this reason, after the work is done, extrinsic motivation causes a new "reward" to be demanded for each task, or it is no longer demanded because the motivation is no longer great enough.

The second dimension is described as positive or negative motivation. Negative motivation describes motivation that is aimed at avoiding negative things.

There is also a suitable school example: A child in the eighth grade knows that there will be trouble at home if he comes home with bad grades. For this reason, he studies a lot. So the child wants to avoid the negative situation that might occur and feels motivated to study for that reason.

Positive motivation, on the other hand, is based on a desired state. A suitable example would be that an adult person wants to stop smoking because she would like to be in better shape again. In addition, she notices herself that the cigarette smoke sticks to her clothes and she would definitely save more money. With this dimension, it is more likely that the adult's motivation will last longer and he will be more successful with his plan. In fact, studies have been able to find out that negative motivation can trigger defiance and have a virtually paralyzing effect on a person.

Short-term versus long-term motivation describes the third dimension of motivational psychology. This dimension simply describes the fact that one should not set oneself too big goals without setting intermediate goals. After all, if you set only one big goal, then it is very likely that you will go through many phases of frustration, which in the end will cause you to give up. However, if you keep setting yourself small intermediate goals and achieve them, you bypass the masses of frustration because you can "refuel" new motivation with each achievement of an intermediate goal.

The last dimension of motivational psychology is conscious or unconscious motivation. Conscious motivation describes the active and deliberate objectives with which one is concerned. The unconscious motivation, on the other hand, describes motives that are located in the unconscious part of the person. This can cause an individual to fail. The unconscious motivation is also called counter-motivation, which can prevent one from implementing a certain conscious goal. An example of this can be found again in school: A student consciously attaches great importance to fairness and justice. For this reason, he wants to help his classmates who are being teased for no reason. His counter-motivation, however, is that he is afraid of being teased himself. Thus, this "unconscious motivation level" can lead to not achieving one's goals. It is striking that especially people who suffer from mental illnesses are affected by this counter-motivation.

Experimental psychology

Experimental psychology" is also called "experimental psychology" and broadly describes the process of gaining knowledge through the execution of subject-related experiments. This experimental psychology already belongs to many psychological topics as a subdiscipline and is considered an important field of investigation. Experimental psychology is also based on medical or general scientific progress, which is why methods and diagnoses can of course be constantly improved. For this reason, this form of psychology is one of the strongest based on progress. Within the framework of experimental psychology, however, there are also many critics. Objections are, for example, that "psychic cannot be measured" and that there should be specifics and limits in experiments.

Clinical psychology

Clinical psychology belongs to the main subject of applied psychology. The task of this psychology is to study fundamentals of mental disorders, taking into account scientific, biological, social, developmental, behavioral, cognitive and emotional aspects.

Normally, clinical psychology was a method of diagnosis, provided that it had been in a clinic or hospital. However, it is still important to mention that medical psychology as well as neuropsychology are strongly connected with clinical psychology. The clinical psychology is used for the analysis of physical or also social, environmental disturbances, whereby by scientific methods for example effect conditions and the behavior on the experience are examined. With its diagnoses, clinical psychology analyzes various behavioral patterns and scientific or even biological processes. However, this sub-theme of applied psychology is not a topic that is treated exclusively in theory, but is also connected with certain practice. Because laboratory experiments are also essential to obtain knowledge in certain aspects.

However, the elaboration and study of mental disorders is likewise only a sub-topic of clinical psychology, because it can actually be fundamentally divided into three theoretical aspects: Methods, Diagnosis, and Treatment. It is not uncommon for clinical psychology to overlap with other topics in psychology.

However, it can be said in general that this psychology is basic research, which compares, researches and examines "disturbed" behavior with "normal" behavior. In addition, this also searches for causes and the development of mental disorders within the framework of further research. Examples of applications of this form of psychology are anxiety disorders or depression.

The psychology of our pets

The question of whether our animals also have a psychology has certainly been asked by many people. Everyone has wanted to know whether their loved one actually has a consciousness similar to ours. Sometimes animals do not behave instinctively, impulsively and guided by primal urges, but show character, love and somehow a human side. The question whether animals also have a consciousness is difficult to answer, because even the consciousness of humans is not clearly definable, but only interpretable from many different approaches in as much detail as possible. One of the cornerstones for the explanation of human consciousness is the sentence "I think, therefore I am" by the French philosopher René Descartes. When a person is said to be "aware of the consequences", for example, this means in subtext that he or she is aware of all possible situations that can occur and then has made a decision with consideration of all contingencies.

A human being is able to control his emotional processes, his thoughts and his actions, to change them and to reflect on them. This is what distinguishes us from animals. At least one should think so, but one hundred percent one cannot claim that. It is still too complex for the present medicine and research to speak an exact judgment about the consciousness of our pets. In fact, research into consciousness is proving to be a real challenge in the animal world. Perhaps the biggest problem is the lack of communication.

With a human being you can communicate by means of our language about behavior, about emotions and about reasons and causes. Animals, however, cannot tell you "That hurt me", "That makes me feel good". Thus, the study of perception in animals is based exclusively on measurements and observations of neurological processes.

But we humans are also so far behind in research because for a very long time the subject had not even been looked at. Something that has been found out, however, is that animals have different traits and not only outside of different species, but also within a race.

These character traits are developed by keeping and raising the animals, as well as how the animals interact with the dogs' mother when they are puppies. In addition, there was an interesting experiment that fueled discussions about the consciousness of animals. The experiment worked on ravens, apes, dolphins as well as elephants. These animals were placed in front of a mirror and had the ability to recognize themselves. This could be found out by placing a blob of color with the animals that they could only see in the mirror. After discovering this color blob, the animals tried to remove it from themselves and not from the mirror image or the like. This has shown that some animals have a consciousness, the only question is on which level the consciousness is located.

But even humans do not have this awareness from the beginning, but learn it only with education. If you hold babies up in front of a mirror, they don't know that they are just mirroring themselves and don't recognize themselves. Because the only thing babies need is the satisfaction of their basic needs.

So the topic is very controversial because it is simply very unexplored and difficult to research. It is possible to prove that our pets are sad or happy by means of chemical substances, but whether the animal itself knows its mood cannot yet be proven. But one thing is clear: it is not impossible!

The Freudian iceberg model

The iceberg model according to Siegmund Freud is a model based on the interaction between psyche and personality. It discusses and describes three essential parts of personality. The three essential aspects of personality are the *conscious*, the *preconscious* and the *unconscious*. This model - hence the name - is visualized with an iceberg floating in water. About twenty percent of the iceberg looks out of the water and eighty percent is below the water surface. The part that stands out of the water is described as the *conscious*, the part that follows it as the *preconscious* and the part that is at the bottom as the *unconscious.*

The conscious part contains all logical, absolute factors. These factors include, for example, data, but also numbers in general and facts. This part is also called the factual level. To the preconscious then rather characteristics count like fears, characteristics of the personality or also suppressed conflicts and important values.

The last part of the personality is the unconscious. This then includes events that have triggered a trauma, for example, the psychosexual development of an individual as well as the instincts with which a person is born. The last two aspects, i.e. the preconscious and the conscious, are subsequently also referred to as the emotional level.

The distribution of these three aspects is, of course, symbolic and wisely chosen. The unconscious is something for which you as an individual have to dig deep. It is often so deep that you can only transport all the things that are in the unconscious part to the conscious or preconscious part with the help of a specialist. For this reason, these two parts of the model are also at the bottom and underwater. The preconscious part is a part which is also under water, but usually does not bring any difficulties. For example, the fear of spiders is something that is usually below the surface, but still obvious to any individual. The conscious part is subsequently above the surface, of course.

With this model, Freud attempts to explain an individual's behaviors and reactions. Namely, the model describes that only about twenty percent of what an individual communicates, whether it is interpersonal or with himself, is based on facts and absolute data, and that the remaining eighty percent is based on experiences and the feelings associated with them. Indeed, he himself describes man as one who is guided by feelings and emotions. He subsequently also supports this thesis or this insight with this iceberg model.

However, the model also has other titles for the respective areas. For example, in other variants, the conscious is called the ego, the preconscious is called the *superego*, and the unconscious is called the *id*. The "I" thus designates the individual as it is. The "superego" is the part of the personality that contains values and morals and the personality aspect "id" describes the basic instincts and the basic drives of a person. This variant of the iceberg model is described in such a way that the id and the superego are in constant conflict, so to speak. The superego, known as the preconscious, is the part that one has learned through society.

That is, through upbringing, an individual knows that one behaves calmly and reasonably in a commuter train because that is how it should be according to social and legal laws. However, it can theoretically happen that the superego gets into a conflict. After all, a human being is designed to reproduce. This means that an individual could get the desire to approach a lady in the suburban train on the basis of his sexual drive and want to reproduce with her. Then the two instances are in conflict, because the learned and the innate are in the way. In such situations, the instance *I* gains in importance, because this instance ultimately decides which action is carried out.

Thus, this instance either tries to decide whether to perform the action of the superego or the id, or decides to mix the two actions and thus compromise. Freud also used this model to describe mental disorders. According to him, a rapist as an extreme example had a pronounced "id" and his drives were in the foreground. In Freud's opinion, however, the whole thing could be counteracted by the "right" education.

40 incredible psychological effects

Following are 40 psychological effects that are not only amazing in the field of psychology, but the knowledge of these effects led to gaining more knowledge about psychology and help in therapies.

The Spotlight Effect

The first effect is the so-called spotlight effect. This effect comes from the field of social psychology and addresses the phenomenon that an individual imagines that other people pay more attention to him than is the case in reality. This often affects people who suffer from severe social phobias.

Self-efficacy expectation

The concept of self-efficacy expectation refers to a person's expectation that he or she will be able to manage his or her own plans on the basis of his or her own competencies. A person who believes that he or she can achieve something through his or her actions, even in difficult situations, has a high SWE. One component of SWE is the belief that, as an individual, one can exert a targeted influence on the world and its events as well as on the course of contemporary history instead of viewing external circumstances such as other people, luck or fundamentally uncontrollable factors as the cause.

Blemish effect

Nobody loves perfect people. The blemish effect refers to the phenomenon that small flaws make things really interesting for us.

Reactance

Psychological reactance is the defensive reaction that occurs when a person is subjected to external or internal restrictions and resistance arises. Reactance is normally triggered by psychological pressure (e.g. threats, prohibitions or similar restrictions). Reactance in the actual sense, however, is not the triggered behavior that arises as a reaction, but the thought that underlies this reaction. Reactance is typically due to the "stimulus of the forbidden". It describes the situation of wanting something even more because it has been forbidden to you.

Pygmalion effect

The Pygmalion effect is when a positive assessment of a person's characteristics is confirmed by another person later on. The well-known example of the teacher-student relationship then works like this: A teacher who is suggested that some students are particularly gifted and predestined to be better than others will unconsciously encourage them in such a way that in the end they also factually increase their performance and thus correspond to his assumption, which he was "talked into" but which had no empirical background for him.

Halo effect

The halo effect (from halo, halo) is a cognitive misperception originating from social psychology, which consists of inferring from known characteristics such as generosity of a person to other positive or even negative unknown characteristics, in the case, for example, while someone who is generous is certainly also tolerant. In the case of a positive bias, one also speaks of the halo effect, and in the case of a negative bias, of the devil's horn effect.

Swimmer Body Illusion

The Swimmer Body Illusion refers to the process in the brain in which a person tries to draw conclusions from cognitive knowledge, but confuses result and selection criterion. The example on which this titling is based is that of a professional swimmer. These have muscular, fit bodies. Compared to professional cyclists or bodybuilders, they appear more natural and coherent because the muscles are more evenly trained. Therefore, the assumption is quickly made that swimming is the perfect sport to get a beautiful body. However, this turns out to be wrong, because the reverse is correct: to be a good swimmer, you already need a balanced trained body and not necessarily the other way around.

Social Loafing

The term social loafing describes a socio-psychological phenomenon that often occurs in group situations. As soon as individuals work collectively with others towards a common goal and their individual performance is not known, their physiological tension is reduced - they feel safe because they believe that their own contribution is not decisive for the result. This relaxation leads to a drop in performance on simple tasks. In contrast, it leads to an increase in performance on difficult tasks, such as new or complex ones. Each individual gets the feeling that his or her part can be decisive and wants it to be, which is perceived as a natural need. Each individual wants to excel.

Socrates irony

Socratic irony is usually understood as a negative self-disguise, e.g. pretending to be stupid, in order to trap one's opponent, who believes himself to be superior. This is done in order to instruct him or to make him think and to show him his assumed superiority and his professionalism.

The Authority Bias

Authority bias is the so-called belief in authority. This effect describes the wordless and uncritical subordination to a person who exudes authority.

The Confirmation Bias

Confirmation bias is also called confirmation bias and refers to the tendency to interpret and interpret information in such a way that an individual always meets his or her own expectations.

The self-serving bias
The self-serving bias is called the self-esteem-serving bias. This means that an individual attributes success to internal causes such as abilities, skills, talent, ambition, etc., and in turn attributes failure to external causes such as chance or the overall situation.

The Outcome Bias
Outcome bias describes the result bias of an individual. This means that an individual tries to evaluate the already made decision in terms of quality despite a known outcome.

The action bias
Action bias refers to the tendency to always take active action, even when one knows that the action may be useless or harmful.

The Liking Bias
The Liking Bias describes the effect that an individual always tries to act reasonably or even "right" because he or she tries to always be liked.

The Survivorship Bias
Survivorship bias describes a bias in favor of the

"survivors". This means that success tends to attract more attention than failure and that unsuccessful individuals are not given the same consideration as successful ones.

The contrast effect

The contrast effect provides a more intense perception of an information by emphasizing a contrast. A common example of this is a reduced article of clothing. A dress that is reduced from 80 euros to 40 euros appears cheaper and better than a dress that has always cost 40 euros.

The hedonistic treadmill

The hedonistic treadmill refers to the effect of returning to a stable standard of living quickly and happily after a stroke of fate (whether that was positive or negative).

The availability error

The availability bias describes the phenomenon that an individual makes up their own statistics based on available information and memory. An example of this is the fear of flying. Most people are afraid of dying during a flight, although it is many times more likely to die in a car accident. This is because an airplane crash is much more present and gruesome in the media.

The possession effect

The possession effect is a phenomenon that occurs when one possesses a good. It means that an object or good is considered more valuable and important when it is owned.

The selection paradox

The choice paradox arises from many different choices. The mass of offers presented to an individual makes it difficult for an individual to decide. The many choices lead to excessive demands.

The Sunk Cost Fallacy Effect

The sunk cost fallacy effect describes the effect that individuals are more likely to see the appeal of continuing a task when money, time, and energy have already been invested and are not recovered.

The Priming Effect

The priming effect means that the very first stimulus and the very first related interpretation is crucial for the rest of an individual's decision.

The illusion of control

The illusion of control describes a person being convinced that they can control something that is demonstrably either not true or not even possible in the first place.

The reciprocity

Reciprocity means mutuality and is the basic principle of human action. Reciprocity provides for what an individual has the desire for. For example, to punish a person who has been unfair and unjust to him.

The player fallacy

The gambler's fallacy describes the phenomenon that an individual believes that coincidences, lucky events, but also unlucky streaks are more likely to occur if they have not occurred for a long time.

The scarcity fallacy

The scarcity fallacy describes the effect that people have a preference for goods that are in limited supply.

The Westermarck Effect

The Westermarck effect refers to the phenomenon that people who have grown up with each other, regardless of relatedness, do not find each other sexually attractive or appealing later in life.

The Dunning-Kruger Effect

The Dunning-Kruger effect means that an individual exhibits the faulty tendency to always overestimate his or her own knowledge and to always underestimate the competencies of others.

The placebo effect

The placebo effect is considered to be one of the most well-known and widespread effects known to mankind and the reason for its functionality cannot be proven. The effect describes the phenomenon that people can "heal themselves" based on their own thoughts. This means that you could sell a candy without medicine to a person with a sore throat and still, if the person takes it regularly, they will no longer have a sore throat simply because they believe it will help.

The nocebo effect

The nocebo effect describes the counterpart to the placebo effect. It describes the phenomenon that people can become ill by their mere imagination. That is, you could give people a piece of candy and say "If you ingest this, you will catch a cold." And it would happen, even though the candy doesn't carry any pathogens.

The Bystander Effect

When the bystander effect occurs, it means that the more people present, the less likely it is that a person will assist in an accident.

The Barnum Effect

This effect describes that an individual interprets generally valid statements in such a way that they apply to the own person. A popular example would be the horoscope. If the zodiac sign Aries says that an Aries is stubborn, then one also interprets this in such a way and arranges experiences and situations in such a way that this characteristic applies.

The superstar effect

The superstar effect describes the phenomenon that one's own performance changes due to the presence of a professional or star.

The Hawthorne Effect

Most recently, the Hawthorne effect describes that people change their behavior provided they know they are under observation and/or participating in a study.

The reverse psychology

Everyone has heard the term reverse psychology. Reverse psychology describes doing the opposite of what is expected. This means that people who are told, for example, not to touch the hot stove top, do it anyway and burn their fingers. Reverse psychology is also part of the Bible in the origin story. It has been forbidden to eat the fruit of the tree in the Garden of Eden, but still the attraction was there to do the forbidden thing. The only question that arises is whether this is simple defiance on the part of a person, because he feels deprived of his freedom by prohibitions, or whether this has a deeper reason. In the field of psychology, the phenomenon that occurs when things are forbidden is called reactance.

Reactance describes a defensive reaction that leads to resistance due to given prohibitions and restrictions. A person often cannot cope with this invisible psychological pressure that robs them of their freedom and therefore changes their motivation to do or not do something as well as their attitude within seconds. For example, if you tell an adult person that they should not become self-employed, they may suddenly gain the motivation to become self-employed, even though they had no intention of doing so before. Reactance thus describes the "attraction of the forbidden".

Therefore, it can be argued that although reactance is very similar to defiance, it is not necessarily the same thing, since reactance usually occurs unconsciously, whereas a pure defiant reaction can be controlled. The occurrence of reactance means in subtext that the importance of actions and information changes, even if one never made use of this "importance" before. So the typical reaction is quasi "I don't care what you say, now I'll do it more than ever!", because the person thus compulsively tries to regain his deprivation of freedom.

Another way to behave in the application of reverse psychology is to regain one's freedom through alternatives. This possibility has the consequence that one is not affected by the prohibitions and is still not restricted in one's freedom of action. Moreover, it has been found that reactance with <u>lethargy</u> and <u>overconformity</u> is among the most important reaction patterns in the area of external pressure or restriction. Nevertheless it is different, how strongly this reactance is pronounced with humans and/or in which form this can be seen. After all, this depends on different factors, such as the extent, i.e. how great the loss of freedom is. Another factor is how much an individual feels his or her own freedom is important, and many others.

According to reactance, an individual theoretically always wants to avoid a loss of control happening, because people usually have negative experiences with loss of control, so the brain often "sounds the alarm" at the hint of it and subconsciously wants to protect you from it.

So reverse psychology is used when you want to get someone into just that attitude. So when you want to motivate someone to get something done, using reverse psychology is very helpful. An example of this would be the following: As a business owner, you advertise voluntary seminars to your employees, but no one signs up, even though they would make the job easier. Now reverse psychology is applied: The entrepreneur writes out seminars that simplify work life with the pressure that the offer will disappear if no one signs up, since no one considers this topic important. This activates reactance and employees will sign up for it.

Effective manipulation and NLP techniques

The psychology of man also includes the power of manipulation techniques and NLP. NLP is the abbreviation of "Neurolinguistic Programming" and includes various techniques and methods that can change mental processes. These methods are based on communication, facial expressions and gestures. NLP is also defined as "the study of the structure of subjective experiences". The basic intention is to find out, analyze and optimize the different factors of a successful therapy.

MANIPULATE THROUGH PLEAS-
ANT ATMOSPHERE

The human psyche can be manipulated by various influences. One of them is manipulation through a pleasant atmosphere. This atmosphere can contain many things that scientifically prove that they calm and relax people. For example, certain colors are among them. For example, the color yellow has an anxiety-fighting and depression-relieving effect on people, the color blue is very familiar, green is harmonious and orange is very mood-lifting.

The use of rain sounds or general nature sounds can also create a stress-free and pleasant atmosphere. And since a person is more likely to be influenced when his basic condition is better, you can actively and consciously manipulate a person into more willingness with a pleasant atmosphere.

MANIPULATION WITH THE HELP OF STRONG EMOTIONS

Another way to manipulate your counterpart is through strong emotions. A classic example here is the shifting of the question of guilt and the shifting of obligations. For example, if person A is dating person B, but has fallen in love with person C, then person A is in an inner conflict, because on the one hand person A does not want to break his principle of fidelity and leave his current partner because of a new person, because otherwise he will have a guilty conscience, but at the same time he still wants to become intimate with person C. This is why person A behaves in such a way toward his partner that he does not feel guilty about it. For this reason, person A behaves towards his partner in such a way that he ends the relationship. Namely, this allows him to blame Person B during arguments and distance himself from it and not feel obligated, even though he manipulated her.

Another example is that person X wants to get more attention from person Y. This is why person X forces tears. For this reason, person X forces himself to cry so that person Y feels obliged to help. This manipulation technique strikes very quickly, because emotions can fundamentally cause chaos. After all, every person always tries to spare the feelings of others or to stand up for his or her own through various considerations.

LIES

Manipulation also works with lies. This is because a false claim can fundamentally make a person think in a different way about a situation because of the false information. This manipulation works very well, of course, if one is not caught lying. However, if one is caught lying, the resulting situation is usually worse than the truth. So lying means risk.

CONCEAL

Concealment is similar to lying, but usually does not lead to major problems when exposed. Nevertheless, concealing information naturally has a manipulative influence. The lack of information ensures that the other person makes decisions without taking all the information into account.

MANIPULATION THROUGH RE-WARDING

Another manipulation technique would be manipulation through rewards. This involves directly addressing the reward. Examples would be, "If you cover my lie, then I'll take you shopping," or even "If you're quiet in class, then you won't get homework." Scientists and physicians have been able to prove that a person can impulsively change their basic attitude or current need. The question of whether the attitude will change always depends only on whether the "exchange" is worthwhile. However, people who want to manipulate you through rewards usually also offer something in return that you don't want to do without.

MANIPULATION BY MEANS OF CRITICISM

However, people can also manipulate other people through criticism. This criticism can then have either a positive or a negative effect on a person. The sentence "When you play the piano, it doesn't sound good" can be received differently by people. Either this sentence can serve as an incentive or it can cause the person to lose his or her enjoyment of playing the piano. So, if you want to manipulate someone through criticism, you have to pay close attention to your choice of words and be able to assess the person well.

CHANGE NUMBERS

You can also manipulate effectively by changing numbers. Falsifying or changing data, facts, statistics and numbers probably has one of the most effective manipulation effects. The rational aspects listed above are in fact fundamentally and comprehensively regarded by people as a "correct" standard and thus never actually questioned.

FOOT IN THE DOOR TECHNIQUE

The "foot in the door" technique means "foot in the door" and describes the willingness of people from whom one has already asked a small favor to do another larger favor. That this technique works was found out by an experiment with signs. This went as follows: First, people were asked at their front door whether they would put up a very small sign in their window. Two weeks later, they were asked if they would put a very large sign in their front yard. It was eventually found that 55% of the people who agreed to put up the small sign were willing to put up the large sign in the yard, while only 17% of the people who were asked directly to put up the large sign complied with the request. This more or less proved that it is possible to manipulate people into "having their foot in the door".

RHETORICAL MEANS

The power of manipulation by rhetorical means is transitional to NLP. Rhetorical means are used for example by politicians to interpret the speech suitably for themselves or also by advertisers and salesmen. There is also a term for it called analogical marking, which describes exactly this use of rhetorical devices and other stylistic devices. This includes, for example, the use of a certain voice pitch or also the setting of pauses in speech and the volume. Also the emphasis of the words as well as the speech speed can take thereby influence on the speech or also on the slogan. Also the conscious employment of Mimik and gestures helps to want to communicate to humans subliminal something and/or to animate humans subliminal to something.

An example of what everyone knows is that supermarket advertisements are often spoken loudly and quickly, while documentaries are often shot at room volume and are also spoken at a normal pace. This is of course because different goals are to be achieved. The only fact is that by using these rhetorical means, the listener is no longer offered an objective view of facts and therefore this technique definitely counts as an effective manipulation or NLP technique.

RAPPORT (NEUROLINGUISTIC PROGRAMMING)

Continuing, we are talking about the NLP techniques. One of them is "Rapport". Rapport describes the contact on the same linguistic level. This serves to the fact that one does not come across incomprehensibly to its counterpart by the assumption of the same level and this is better understood. It creates trust and helps through the same language that the other person understands something through the use of "his language", which he would not have understood before and one can therefore convince this person faster or better.

MIRRORING (NEUROLINGUISTIC PROGRAMMING)

The so-called mirroring describes almost the same as rapport, only that it is not only verbal adaptation, but also non-verbal adaptation. This means that people always try to imitate the gestures and facial expressions as well. This imitation of gestures and facial expressions in combination with the imitation of speech has a very sympathetic effect on the person opposite, because he can identify himself.

LEADING (NEUROLINGUISTIC PROGRAMMING)

Leading is also part of NLP and describes the leading of conversations. This is achieved through mirroring and rapport.

REFRAMING (NEUROLINGUISTIC PROGRAMMING)

Refraiming in this context means as much as "giving a framework". This means that new behavior, new meanings, new reactions as well as new beliefs can be developed.

Change habits

Change habits. This statement is easier said than done, but it is an essential step for a person's psyche. In order for a person who is not particularly happy due to life circumstances etc. to become happy again, he must change and reformulate his habits and his associated attitudes and beliefs.

For example, if it has become a habit to get up only 20 minutes before work starts every morning, even though the individual is annoyed every morning because he or she cannot eat breakfast, then the individual should change just that. One could change the habit to shower in the morning followed by breakfast. Because even though it may seem rather hard to implement this at first, it is just a matter of *habit*. In addition, new habits help to celebrate new periods of life in silence. Symbolically, you get yourself a new stage and show yourself open to new things.

For this reason, you should also restructure your habitual beliefs. Beliefs are statements and convictions that are stuck in you without you knowing exactly where this opinion comes from. An example of such a belief would be, "All bosses are arrogant, so I never want to be one." A positive restructuring would be, "Being a boss is definitely a challenge, I'd like to be on that side of the table." Even such a restructuring does not work overnight, of course, but it is purely a matter of getting used to it and is very important if you also want to actively change something in your behavior.

So an individual's beliefs include things, expectations, priorities, opinions, and more that we think are true based on upbringing, experience, media, and so on. These sentences, with which an individual represents his opinions and views, have something to do with which truth one believes in consciously or even subconsciously. For example, just because parents said "You don't talk about money" doesn't mean that it is a general topic that is taboo. You just think it because that's how you were taught. And the same goes for phrases that have something to do with an individual personally, such as saying "You can't play the piano."

Because the negative side effect of such statements is that at some point you start to take this sentence for yourself and then say to yourself "I can't do that". And that's also where the key of these beliefs lies. You have to learn to restructure and rephrase this. Positive thoughts have to be consolidated as well as the willingness to question one's own opinion once and to change it if necessary. Of course, it is anything but easy to restructure the beliefs one carries within oneself and to change one's habits, but if it helps the psyche to feel better, these questionings and changes are definitely worth it.

This restructuring of beliefs and habits also has something to do with the generic term neurolinguistic programming. Habits and beliefs influence everyday thinking and subconsciously influence decisions and behavior. And by actively changing them, you can "reprogram" your brain to think in different ways.

Visualization as an aid to achieving goals

The key to achieving one's goals in the field of psychology is based on the concept of visualization, which describes the need to keep the problem in mind and the corresponding goal. It is important to be clear about where exactly the problem lies. You should know what is bothering you, because only with this knowledge you can actively work on it. But as soon as you have visualized the problem, you can start visualizing the goals. That is, one should always answer the question "What do I want? What do I need? What would make me happy from the bottom of my heart?". After you have been able to answer this, you can actively deal with the path that will take you to your goal. As already mentioned, it is important to set realistic intermediate goals. But this is not the only thing you need to visualize. In psychology, it is important to know oneself and not to stand in one's own way during the learning process. Especially the inner strength of an individual is important and essential as well as the social environment.

Close

In conclusion, psychology contains countless super-topics and sub-topics with various complex ramifications that are very difficult to understand. However, the psyche of a person is incredibly important and should be taken care of by each individual. Maintaining inner strength, maintaining self-confidence and dealing with frustration are the most important points to consider. Moreover, in conclusion, it can be said that the various branches of psychology have always wanted at least one thing: Explaining human behavior in a wide variety of contexts.